Say It When You Mean It

Poetic Expressions by A Non-Poet

Raman K. Attri

Rayan & Rayman Imprints, Singapore
Rayan-rayman@outlook.com

Copyright © 2019 by Raman K. Attri and Rayan & Rayman Imprints. All Rights Reserved. No part of this publication may be reproduced, distributed, or transmitted in any form or by any means, including photocopying, recording, or other electronic or mechanical methods, without the prior written permission of the publisher, except in the case of brief quotations embodied in critical reviews and certain other noncommercial uses permitted by copyright law. Write to the publisher/author for seeking explicit permission for any reproduction, inclusion or usage in another publication. Provide an appropriate reference/citation to this publication when posting brief excerpts or quotations from this text on social media channels. For seeking permissions to use the poems, in full or partial, in this book in any online or printed greeting cards or merchandise, please contact the publisher at Rayan-rayman@outlook.com.

ISBN: 978-981-14-0827-4 (e-book)
ISBN: 978-981-14-0828-1 (paperback)
First Published: December 2018
Lead author: Raman K. Attri
Cover graphics and design by Raman K. Attri
Published by Rayan & Rayman Imprints
Published at Singapore
Printed in the United States of America

National Library Board, Singapore Cataloguing in Publication Data:
Name(s): Attri, Raman K., 1973-
Title: Say it when you mean it : poetic expressions by a non-poet / Raman K. Attri.
Description: Singapore : Rayan & Rayman, [2019]
Identifier(s): OCN 1089646505 | ISBN 978-981-14-0827-4 (e-book) | ISBN 978-981-14-0828-1 (paperback)
Subject(s): LCSH: Attri, Raman K., 1973- | Poetry.
Classification: DDC 821--dc23

A collection of simple poems and verses for greeting cards written between 1990 to 2004.

To some amazing souls who deserved more than words and promises –
Neeru 'Jaan', Shailja 'Senorita', Laxmi 'Luvmi'

Contents

About the Book ix
About the Author xi
THE SIGHT 1
What Are You Neptune Girl? 3
I wonder What Is in Your Mind 6
Crossing Like Strangers 8
THE LOVE 11
Power Of Love 13
Ever Since I've Known You 15
Something Unknown 16
THE PROMISE 17
If I Could Tell 19
I'll Hold You 20
If You Are On My Side In This Fight 22
Creature Of Love 24
You'll Never Leave Alone 26
Listen To My Heart 27
I'm Sensitive To All Your Tears And Fears 29
THE MEMORIES 33

I still cherish memories of those times...35

Remembering You...37

You Mean So Much To Me..39

Let Us Begin A New Beginning Again..41

THE ADIEU...43

Come, Let Us Embrace And Part..45

Time Changes - Comes The Seasons..48

Call Me No More..50

I'll Live In Your Soul...52

THE CYCLE..55

I Need A Friend..57

Once Again..59

Suppressed..61

THE LESSONS..63

Lessons Of Assertiveness...65

Sensitive to All..67

World Is Not Lost...70

About the Book

This book is a collection of very simple expressions written and presented in the form of the poetic verses. This collection of 27 poems included in this book is basically a spin-off of greeting cards written by the author for some of the special people in his life. These poems were originally drafted between the year 1990 to 2004 which represented phases in author's life which every normal boy would go through in his twenties towards adulthood. The work presented in this book, by no means, is claimed to be of poetical or literary standard. It is just an attempt to tell the world that a simple expression or thought if you mean to say it with all your heart, can and will become a piece of poetic expression.

The poems in the book are presented in seven sections: "The Sight" section include the poetic work to express what it may feel like when one sees the most special person for the first time. That's the beginning, though not all first sights transient into love. The next section "The Love" includes the poems expressing the transformation one may feel during the love. "The Promise" section presents the expressions that signify the promises we tend to make when we are in love. "The Memories" section is meant for those poetic expressions which express how one may feel while away from his/her beloved ones. "The Adieu" section is an inevitability that occurs in any relationship and is expressed through some poems in this section. "The Cycle" represents those poetic expressions that life does not stop at one place or one person. The cycle starts again, but it does leave some lessons. "The Lessons" section includes some general poetic verses written at a spur of the moment.

A Note to Readers

The poems are written by an ESL author and are presented as-it-is the way these were written originally 25 years before the publication. Though modern word processing resources, experienced editors and two decades of author's experience would have allowed editing, rephrasing, corrections, and re-writing of these expressions again, the author chose to retain the original innocence and simplicity in word choices, phrases, structure and language used. Readers are requested to read and appreciate the works in the light of above.

About the Author

Raman K. Attri is an international management consultant by profession and an engineer by background. He is author of over twelve books in management, leadership including few poetry and arts books. The writing was his childhood interest that he continued to pursue it in various forms and shapes. During early school and college years, he wrote verses and poetic pieces for greeting cards, which eventually became poetic expressions. His artistic interests include poetry in English and Hindi, portraits, painting and real-life short stories, several of which are being transformed into published work now.

THE SIGHT

Say It When You Mean It

WHAT ARE YOU NEPTUNE GIRL?

15-Sep-1998

What are you – Neptune girl?
A cozy, calm haven of tranquillity;
soft, dreamy and naive;
very delicate and eternally feminine;
a pretty, helpless creature;
every man's sweetheart.

What are you – Neptune girl?
Strange lights in greenish-brown eyes;
who want to see only the goods,

Say It When You Mean It

tiny fragile and exquisitely shaped hands;
a soft silky touch of your skin;
fine wary light hairs,
swinging over your naïve face.

What are you - Neptune girl?
a shy smile on your lips;
but demure vulnerable to conflicts;
when reality becomes too harsh,
you hide behind your dreams.

What are you - Neptune girl?
Living in this scary world;
you carry little protection,
a cloak of sophisticated veneer;
worn to shield your anxiety
from this harsh world.

What are you - Neptune girl?
sentimental when you're hurt,
you cry endless.

Say It When You Mean It

you pour your tenderself out,

writing lovely songs and lyrics,

woven with secret messages underneath.

What are you ~ Neptune girl?

Credits: Inspired by Linda Goodman's Love Signs for Pisces woman.

I wonder What Is in Your Mind

12-Jan-1993

So many persons I know
      and so many I've seen.
But no one like you,
      truly I've ever seen.

Sitting in a group of people,
      still you look distances apart.
As if annoyed with yourself,
      strangely detached and distant.

Soft pinkish lips tremble to speak
      but nip them under your teeth.

Say It When You Mean It

Your lovely eyes feel like in a dream,
      yet, seems to be devoid of a dream.

I don't see you waiting
      for any special someone.
You've a heart beating
      which beats for no one.

You touch us like a cool breeze,
      yet, it does not belong to one.
You remind me of a wandering cloud
      that's waiting to rain on someone.

Sometimes look lost
      and sometimes trying to find.
I think of you quite often
      I wonder what is in your mind.

CROSSING LIKE STRANGERS

1-Jan-1993

Just wanting to say I got attracted to you,
On the very first sight.
I urged talking to you for days,
And share what's in my heart.
It's true never talked to
And we have never met.
Though I feel I know you,
You don't know me yet.
Almost like some strangers,
Crossed each other on the street.
Never could my eyes fail to tell -

Say It When You Mean It

How much I'm longing to meet.
So long I have been longing
To say few words to greet.
To steal your smiles,
That makes me feel great.

THE LOVE

POWER OF LOVE

In my heart –
I feel free;
On my dry lips –
A warm smile's dance;
In my eyes –
Heavenly confidence;
On my ugly face –
A glowing psychic light;
In my talking –
A hope of tomorrow;
In my outlook –
A positive sense about the world;
In my feelings –

Say It When You Mean It

A strange optimism that surrounds;

My attitude –

Is of a winner of the game;

My days –

Are full of never-ending energy;

In my inner self

Got over my inhibitions and fears;

Such is the power of love – perhaps.

Ever Since I've Known You

Ever since I've found you beside me,
I've become more caring somewhere inside me.
Never was I so sensitive to the persons around me.
Never was the world such a different place to me.
Never was I so simple to complex things around me.
Never was I so aware of persons so dearly love me.
Never was I so seeing things clearly inside me.
Your affection is making a beautiful change in me.

Something Unknown

Let there be a little enhance,
free from fear of the domestic way,
free from worries of a workday.

Not in the traditional way,
something is yet to appear one day,
with riddles of love, life, and joy.

Here in the intensity of life,
between you and me, something still unknown,
which neither you nor I can define.

∞ ∞ ∞

THE PROMISE

If I Could Tell

9-Mar-1993

How much delighted I'll be to get you,
Your friendship, your nearness and your love too.
How my life has changed because of you;
If I could, I would tell you one day.
Forget the world, we need not to care;
They envy the love because they don't know.
Perhaps life wants me to come to you.
If I could, I would tell you one day.

I'll Hold You

15-Oct-1999

I'll hold you
Until the end;
When worried,
I'll cheer you up.
When wrong,
I'll mold you.
When lost,
I'll find you.
I'll be there for you
and care enough for you.
I'll never let you part,
for you're always in my heart.

Say It When You Mean It

I wish
I could be there for you
when you need me.
I'll hold you
Until the end.

∞ ∞ ∞

If You Are On My Side In This Fight

19-Oct-1999

I'll take the world on stake for you.
      I'll play the clown for you.
I'll change the rules for you.
      Just say anything and I'll do it for you.

I told you that I need you;
      a thousand times and why.
I played the fool for you,
      please don't ever say goodbye.

I told you I'll get you.
      One day will be brighter.

Say It When You Mean It

I'll fight with the world for you,
> for your love for me is that would matter.

If we try together,
> we'll not find fear or dread feeling.

In the deepest of love,
> once again, we will start living.

The future we believed in
> will reveal a joyful face.

And the dreams we believed in,
> will shine its grace.

If you are on my side in this war,
> it'll take time but one day I'll join you.

Then there won't be any need to get hurt,
> because so much I will love you.

CREATURE OF LOVE

1999

When you see these tiny fish,

pushing hard on the glass walls to find their way;

> Think of me,

> I would be restless for you too same way.

To come closer to you someday,

In the hope of the brightest day;

> Think of me,

> Somewhere I'd be trying hard too same way.

Waiting to get you, my dear, someday.

In the deepest oceans of love for you!

Think of me,
I would be swimming around too same way;

You'll Never Leave Alone

17-Feb-1993

Just call me when you can,
you will find me near every time.
Come may alone,
but you'll never leave alone.
Even if you betray,
never shall I complain,
Break your promises,
if you wish you can.
Never will I do the same,
Never leave you back again.

∞ ∞ ∞

Listen To My Heart

1999-2000

Whenever the chimes tinkle together,
the sound that emits,
beneath those musical tones,
listen saying to you, sweetheart -
I love you, infinite.

If a cool breeze around the room
makes them chime,
be certain to hear the voice therein
listen saying to you, sweetheart -
I want to feel you warm and tight.

Say It When You Mean It

When the day seems dim and sad,

listen to the calm sound,

it'll make you feel bold,

Listen saying in your ear, sweetheart -

hold the love for the day we meet.

I'm Sensitive To All Your Tears And Fears

8-Aug-1998

I may feel weak, hurt or emotional

but indifferent to you – never.

    Despite constant reprimands

    from your worried wears.

    I'll continue to treat

    as mine, all stresses of you bear.

I may feel weak, hurt or emotional

but indifferent to you – never.

    Your sad saga will always make me

spend sleepless nights.
I'd kept my face averted,
lest you should see my tears;
because I'm sensitive to all
your tears and fears.

I may feel weak, hurt or emotional
but indifferent to you – never.
I'll try to take away the hell,
and every day's agony you live.
My heart will continue rejoicing
with all your good and bad actions;
keep on shedding tears with you,
and consider your fears and tears as mine.

I may feel weak, hurt or emotional
but indifferent to you – never.
If you are sad ever,
I'll also experience the blues.
But a song on my lips,
just a glimpse of your face would bring.

I may feel weak, hurt or emotional

but indifferent to you – never.

> Credits: Inspired by an unknown
> source/ anonymous work in late 1980s.

THE MEMORIES

I STILL CHERISH MEMORIES OF THOSE TIMES

10-Feb-1993

It's true we're miles and miles apart.
Still, often I remember you in my thought.
    Life is hard and tough at times,
    What we tackle day and night.

Sometimes we are helpless,
And sometimes lost for a while.
    On every such a moment,
    I wanted so much to talk to all the time.

I wished to see you,

Say It When You Mean It

but I couldn't come your way.
    I wished to write to you,
    But something came on my way.

Now so many persons I know
but nobody like you I've seen.
    I've come to realize that
    To each other, how much we mean.

It was never obvious to me,
Until the day we parted our paths.
    With all your fun and charm,
    Let's try to relive our past that we lost.

I hope you'll forget that has gone,
And would be back to me once again.
    With a newness in our relationship,
    On the grounds of a new understanding grown.

Remembering You

 29-Jan-1993

It has been a while we sat together,
and shared the joy and woes together.

The times of warmth and care,
sweet were those gone yesteryears.

I embrace the memories of those times,
Still, I relive those precious moments.

I still remember those days,
when we lived the moment of enjoys.

Say It When You Mean It

Sometimes I get excited and gloomy sometimes,
when we shared ideas and thoughts so fine.

I wished to write to you day and night,
but something wasn't in favor of mine.

It is true we are now far apart,
you've to believe, I did not forget you all this while.

How can I forget you, so good friend of mine?
Hope you'll forgive me and good to me again.

You Mean So Much To Me

5-Jan-1993

You mean so much to me...
      though I hardly ever let you know,
I think of you almost every day,
      and feel your love in its rich glow.

You mean so much to me...
      for I adore the time the way we share.
the true meaning of growing
      in the light and warmth of bond we bear.

Say It When You Mean It

You mean so much to me...
      when I think of the pleasant days gone by,
when I imagine about the good times yet to unravel,
      in the moments beyond today along the way.

You mean so much to me...
      I know whom to turn to and trust,
when I need my dearest friend,
      who will soothe me with her loving touch.

You mean so much to me...
      I would like to give you all I could,
in return of everything you gave me
      the best of everything that you could.

Let Us Begin A New Beginning Again

We really had the moments of joys,
When we indulged in long talks for hours.

    Sometimes annoyed with each other,
    And sometimes teasing each other.

Waiting eagerly to see and talk together,
Moments of loving and caring for one another.

    At times when we ignored each other,
    Still so memorable the days we had together.

It has been a while we sat together,

And shared the joys and woes together.

    I wish we could have lived longer together,
Perhaps it would've made a different world altogether.

THE ADIEU

Come, Let Us Embrace And Part

9-Apr-1993

On this last night of our relationship,

let's recall everything,

our laughs and weeps,

over the nights we spent,

dreaming of the future in our sleeps.

Let's recall

the days full of joys

and miseries we cried over.

Say It When You Mean It

Recall everything,

You and I can before we depart,

and then preserve those memories

in our mind for years.

You say,

let's shake hands forever,

cancel all vows taken together,

and when we may meet ever again,

we won't keep a former hatred retain.

Be it that we don't ignore

each other as if never met before.

Since there is no help,

come, let's embrace and part.

You don't get any more of me.

and I won't get any part of you.

We know it'll not be easy,

still, let us take our ways.

Goodbye to you

and wish you a bright life,

and thanks for so much

what you've offered to my life.

TIME CHANGES - COMES THE SEASONS

2-Apr-1993

Time changes come the seasons.
Everyone doesn't know the reasons.

Here comes the life and here it flies.
Here it comes in relationships and ages in years.
Passes in our acts and sustains in our memories,
The pure, rich and sweet glories.

Among those precious moments,
One day in my life is the pleasantest.
And it is the day when we met,
Reminding me of the time we spent.

Say It When You Mean It

There've been times we're humble,
Shared each other's anguish and trouble.
Indeed, there're the times we argued endlessly,
And teasing each other carelessly.

A childish fun between you and me,
A fun made up of love, affection and glee,
Which I had with you every day and night.
The memoirs I held like pearls in the oyster.

All your memories flashing on my mind this day,
I wish you the best of luck wherever you stay.
Relationships and all go through some challenges,
May destiny be cordial to you during these changes!

Time will keep on changing, coming be the seasons,
Neither you nor I'll ever know the reasons.

Credits: Inspired by an unknown source/ anonymous work.

Call Me No More

16-Feb-1993

Call me no more from the past,
No more give me the gloomy cast,

The thoughts I don't want to adopt.
To the time that is lost.

Yet remain some faint impressions on the track
Often trying to drag me back.

Cling no more to what's gone,
The things which had driven me insane.

Say It When You Mean It

Long gone is who I was,
Give me no more songs so sad.

Forgot all that didn't matter again,
No hatred no grudged to retain.

I'll Live In Your Soul

25-Aug-1998

If it happened in reality
      Or it was just a dream.
I kept falling deeper into
      almost black stream;

Something strange
      Entered this surround;
I looked at the scene,
      Rubbed my eyes in astound.

In the frosty mist and twilight,
      An unearthly light was moving;
Followed by a radiant aura,

Say It When You Mean It

This wonder kept on shining;

A distinguished figure of a woman
      I noticed as I gazed at it in excitement.
Enveloped in all silvery outlook,
      Of some heavenly enlightenment.

She kept coming closer and closer;
      Her face and eyes were gleaming brilliantly.
Floating and walking in the air slowly,
      Smoothly and passionately.

She looked at me with immense love,
      And at that moment I wanted to die.
What a blue shinning joy,
      Flowing out of her eyes.

It is my beloved's naïve soul
      Realizing that froze me for a while.
What a freshness and innocence
      Shone in her smile.

Say It When You Mean It

She raised her hands
></br>In careful tender motion.
And said - I came for you,
></br>For your obsession and passion.

If it could go on till eternity,
></br>I'd have loved to remain senseless.
If time could have stopped,
></br>My beloved's union would sustain endless.

Said she - I would stay forever,
></br>In your soul, in your smile shall I bloom.
Swallowed in the mist,
></br>She vanished into the gloom.

∞ ∞ ∞

THE CYCLE

I Need A Friend

9-Jan-1993

I need a friend,
    Someone who would know,
      In my self-doubts,
    Why I'm feeling low.

I need a friend,
     Who could keep hope,
    Ask me no more,
  What I am going to do.

I need a friend,
    Preaches me no more,
  Someone who would understand,

Say It When You Mean It

What I am going through.

Credits: Inspired by Glenn Frey's "The One You Love" lyrics.

∞ ∞ ∞

ONCE AGAIN

24-Mar-1993

I have fallen in love many times
Some could work, some just failed.
Every new hurt
Fetched me a new pain.
Every such pain,
Brought with it a new oath.
That never to fall in love again.

But then, I meet love again.
My resolutions get turned around.
What is right?
What is wrong?
All seems not to matter anymore.

Say It When You Mean It

The sweetness of newly found love,
Forgotten are the old pains.

Ready to face the end
I know it will happen again.
But then, time will
make me fall in love again.

SUPPRESSED

I covered them,
and I just crushed them;
The feelings –
I never could outburst them.

I lived in
a world of imagination,
hardly getting closer
to the realization.

That now I'm torn
and cannot take it anymore,
I need a companion
and something more.

I want to express
and want to share about myself,
joys and woes of my life
the experience of the inner self.

THE LESSONS

Lessons Of Assertiveness

29-Aug-1998

You may not have listened me say it too often,
That unconsciously, you've taught me a lesson;

The lesson of realities and truths untold;
The crimpled frailties of life, a heart can't hold.

The expression of anger from words to practice;
The art of genuine agitation against injustice;

With you, I understood why one must have arrogance;
When treated badly by people after you were gone.

Say It When You Mean It

Forgiveness work sometimes, bygones are not gone.
One must push back unjust criticism and put-downs.

Art of being assertive, fighting back and stand;
For our rights, feelings, freedom, and demand.

Your bubbling zeal for achieving greater success,
I feel is the essence of life for its fullness.

Your rare art of living life lively and being cheerful;
Gives me a ray of inspiration to be joyful.

SENSITIVE TO ALL

8-Mar-1993

I cannot blame anyone,
For the fault lies within me.
It's no one's problem but mine
If I let people hurt me.
I cannot hold it against anyone,
For being what they are.
Trample on my feelings
And let people hurt me.
It includes my friends,
Because they matter.
And so are their actions and words,
Their fears and tears,
Their successes and failures.

Say It When You Mean It

I am sensitive to everything of theirs.
Why do you let things affect you?
Why don't you just ignore them?
Despite constant reprimands
from my worried well-wishers,
I continued to treat,
As if mine, were the problems of theirs.
Because someone's sad saga
Had me spent sleepless nights.
And someone else's pain and anguish,
haunted me for a long.
I felt their hurt as if it was mine,
And share the hell in which they live
But I go about my day,
Letting every little thing bother me.
I also experience the blues,
If sad are the people around.
And someone's happy smiling face,
Brings a song to my lips.
But sometimes I ponder -
Does all this matter to them at all?

Say It When You Mean It

In this world of make belief,
Good intentions are not appreciated.
And thoughtful gestures are laughed at
But my tender inner declared -
I will continue to rejoice
to their failure and successes,
Shed tears with them,
And listen to their fears.

∞ ∞ ∞

WORLD IS NOT LOST

24-Aug-1998

They let me go to earth
      and find out what life means.
I came, grew and observed
      life in many forms.

In the childhood
      life was a fun, I thought.
Soon I grew up a little more
      and became conscious somewhat.

A lot of images were constructed
      and a lot were broken.
A lot of views were rectified

Say It When You Mean It

and a lot more were shaken.

I faced tough people sometimes
      and huge affection too.
And all hypocrites and traditions,
      jealously and malignancy too.

I thought those were real faces
      what people presented.
Looked closer and how ugly,
      ravage and twisted they turned.

I felt nauseated through
      my new visions of starkness.
Could the faces so sweet and soft
      hide so much bitterness?

Not to say that every face
      I see is that of sin and devil.
I see an angel in every demon
      and affection and humanity as well.

I see empathy and love
> of common people's soulful eyes.

Lovely smile in every frown,
> makes every miserable feel much better.

I see silent tears shed
> by someone for a closed beloved.

I even see people share
> with each other a warm personal smile.

Such fortunate ones
> fill everyone with eternal optimism and hope.

If there are still such benign beings
> the world is not lost.

"Say It When You Mean It"
The title is inspired by some unkept promises, by us or by others!

From the same author

Kuch Kahi Kuch Ankahi Batein

Timeless Untold Expressions

Collection of poems in Hindi
Available in Ebook and paperback formats
ISBN 978-981-14-0826-7 (ebook), 978-981-14-0825-0 (paperback)
Write to rayan-rayman@outlook.com to place the order

Front cover: Illusion of Reality, painted year 2011
Back cover: A little of something, painted year 2004
Portraits drawn by Raman K. Attri
Front back cover art by Raman K. Attri
Copyrights © 2019

www.ingramcontent.com/pod-product-compliance
Lightning Source LLC
LaVergne TN
LVHW041540070526
838199LV00046B/1755